Ballin'

On A

Budget

Smart Money Moves To Enhance Your Savings

Angel Radcliffe

For bulk ordering please email Info@MissRMBA.com or contact;

CAS Consultants

3900 Teleport Blvd #141381

Irving TX 75014

Dedication

This book is dedicated to every person trying to find their way towards financial freedom, to the person who is living check to check and believes there is 'no way out', to the college graduate drowning in debt, to the single parent 'barely making it', to the families who can't seem to find the 'extra cash', to the 'successful one' in the family who everyone borrows money from, to the person who fears the next payday loan, to the person who is living above their means, to the person who is ready to take the next step towards their financial goals.
I salute you, this is a step worth celebrating.

About The Author

Angel Radcliffe,MBA is a Public Speaker, Author, Motivator & Entrepreneur. She holds an MBA in finance from Strayer University & has 10+ years in Corporate America in the areas of; Finance, Accounting & Technology. She is the owner of CAS Consultants, a boutique consulting firm in Dallas, TX focusing on 'Empowering Entrepreneurs Through Financial Management'. A continued advocate of philanthropy, Ms. Radcliffe is always finding a way to give back to the community, she is currently entering into her 8th consecutive year on the Board of Directors for a local non-profit as Finance Chair & is driven towards starting a non-profit in the near future. Ms. Radcliffe is a recipient of the National Financial Educators Award & is dedicated to educating the community on Financial Literacy – Credit & Budget Management for consumers & Small Business Finance.

Table Of Contents

What is a budget?

A budget is a set amount of money to spend based on NET INCOME and can be split into categories to accommodate you.

BUDGET OVERVIEW TASKS.......

- Review 3 months of bank statements

- Review 3 months of credit card statements

- Review your interest rates on any loans/credit cards

- Identify your #1 expense for your needs & wants

- Identify at least 1 item you can remove from spending

- Identify at least 1 item in which you could have price matched/saved on

"If You Can't Control Your Money,
Making More Won't Help !!"

-Angel Radcliffe

5 REASONS YOU NEED A BUDGET

-

1. *Savings* – You want to be sure you are saving for a 'rainy day' /emergency fund. You may also want to set savings goals for a new car or vacation.

2. *Retirement*- Aside from your savings accounts, you want to distribute monies to your 401k/IRA accounts for your retirement

3. *Stop Overspending* – Being on a budget gives you financial control and will keep you from overspending.

4. *Less Stress* – Once you have a budget in place, you now know where your money is going. You may also be saving more, in turn causing less stress.

5. *Reduce Arguments/Reason for Divorce*- Financial issues is a top reason for divorce. When couples are in control of their money, there are less arguments.

Chapter 1

GET ON A BUDGET 50/30/20 STYLE

Are you on a budget? The first step to increasing your savings is learning money management and budgeting. What's a budget anyhow? A budget is a set amount of money to spend and can be split into categories to accommodate you. When you put yourself on a budget, you keep yourself from overspending and learn where your money is going by tracking your purchases.

Your personal budget should be split into 3 major categories; Needs, Wants & Savings. When setting a budget, you always want to refer to your **NET** income (What you bring home) as opposed to GROSS (What you make overall) The budget only makes sense to what is being deposited in your bank account.

The 50/30/20 Rule is one practical way to get you in high gear towards saving & financial management.

Let's see the 50/30/20 Rule in Action

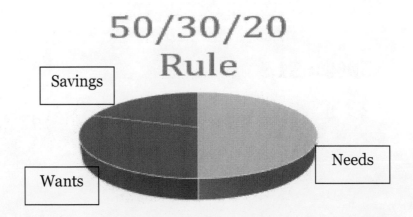

Let's say your NET Income is **$3,000** a month; No more than 50% of your net income should be spent on **NEEDS**, this maximum would equate to $1,500. ($3,000 * .50% =$1,500) Needs include, what you need to survive, Rent/Mortgage, Insurance, Groceries, Car payment, Gas, etc.

The 30% category is your **WANTS**, a want is an expense which is not necessarily needed to survive, wants include, vacation, shopping, entertainment, etc. If you are bringing home $3,000 a month, your wants should not exceed $900, ($3,000 * .30% =$900)

At bare minimum, you should be **SAVING** 20% of your NET income. If you are bringing home $3,000, $600 ($3,000* 20% = $600) would go to your savings account following this rule. You can always choose to save more if you can and spend less, which is always wise.

50/30/20 Rule in Action

- Net Income = **$3,000** per month

50/30/20 Rule

- **50% = $1,500**
- **30% = $900**
- **20%= $600**

Needs • Wants • Savings •

Refer to the **Appendix** to complete the 50/30/20 worksheet.

Ballin' On A Budget Question

What is your #1 Expense in the Needs & Wants Category?
Are you able to reduce the expense? What are you willing to
sacrifice to save more money ?

_____

_____

_____

_____

_____

_____

_____

_____

_____

_____

_____

_____

_____

Chapter 2

MINT (NO CANDY HERE)

Are you ready to start your budget? Once you have decided to create a budget, write your financial goals down on paper. You always want to write out your goals before putting them into action. Of course, keeping up with tasks on paper can be complicated, so you now are ready to put your budget into electronic format.

Mint.com is a FREE consumer resource which allows you to track your spending habits through your bank accounts & credit cards. You can set up a budget, set alerts when you are nearing your budget and so forth. A top recommendation for someone new to budgeting.

Mint is available via the web as well as an app download on Android/IOS.

Mint allows you to not only set a budget but allows the user to track categorized spending. This comes in handy for the person who impulse buys or can never figure out 'where the money went'

Let's take a look at a few of the capabilities you have using Mint.

Set A Budget: Mint allows the user to set a budget by setting limits on each spending category.

If you are setting a budget for the first time and you may find yourself updating your limits after the first few months. Your budget is set on your goals as well as spending habits.

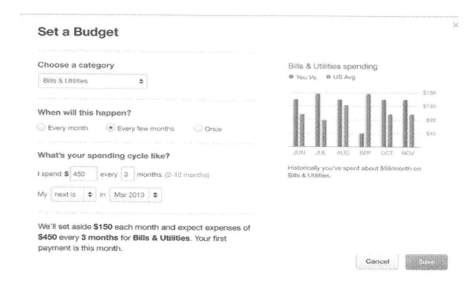

View Spending By Category: For the visual person, you can view your spending in categories on a pie chart. This makes it easy to compare where your money is going. Once you see how much money are spending on frivolous items compared to your needs, the saying 'old habits die hard' comes into play.

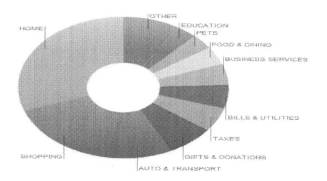

Budget Alerts: Once you set your budget spending limits, Mint allows the user to view your spending and savings progress. If you are approaching a spending limit, color codes are in place to alert you as well as email and text alert options. Yellow means you are very close to your budget, Green means you are below your spending limit, while Red indicated you are over your budget for the particular category. If you choose to log onto the app a few times a week, the color codes will keep you aware of where you stand. If you prefer email and text alerts instead of logging in to the app or website, you will receive notifications to keep you from overspending.

Income
$2,715 so far
of $3,000

Spending
$774 spent
of $1,340

Income	$2,715 *of* $3,000
Auto & Transport: **Auto Insurance**	$0 *of* $100
Auto & Transport: **Auto Payment**	$189 *of* $300
Bills & Utilities: **Mobile Phone**	$0 *of* $150
Education: **Student Loan**	$0 *of* $240
Entertainment	$0 *of* $30
Food & Dining: **Groceries**	$31 *of* $160
Food & Dining: **Restaurants**	$180 *of* $150

Ballin' On A Budget Question

Have you put your budget in writing? Start thinking about what items you should budget for, this includes savings !! Use your notes here as well as the worksheets from the **Appendix** to create your budget.

_____

_____

_____

_____

_____

_____

_____

_____

_____

_____

_____

_____

_____

_____

Chapter 2 Tasks

- Set up an account on Mint.com

- Download the Mint App

- Use your written budget to create an electronic budget

- Be sure to review your budget and spending habits on a regular basis, as some items classified as 'needs' may change overtime. You can adjust your budget accordingly.

Chapter 3

THOSE POINTS REALLY ADD UP

Traveling can be one of the best forms of relaxation, it can also put a damper on your savings. Before planning any vacation, even a trip home to family. Ask yourself the budget questions 'Can I Afford it?" Be smart about your travel arrangements, let's see what cost are typically included in travel:

- Airfare

- Hotel

- Rental Car

- Food

- Entertainment Expenses

- Airport Parking / Taxi

Many are unaware of the major advantages in joining a rewards program with hotels, airlines, etc. Each time you fly, rent a car, or make everyday purchases, you could earn points towards your next flight or rental car which could turn out to be free !! Yes FREE, I have personally taken trips in which I used points to purchase my airline ticket, hotels and rental car, only leaving the minimal expense of food and travel to/from the airport as well as baggage fees. Even if you are not a regular for a particular hotel brand or airline, sign up with each brand, you never know when you will be a second time customer.

There are many brands known for their points programs, below is a list of a select few;

- Southwest Airlines

- American Airlines

- Marriot

- Hyatt

- Alamo Rent A Car

Credit Card companies also participate in reward programs, be sure to check out rewards you may earn and convert from spending.

Let's take a look at how easy it is to convert points to free travel perks.

Depending on the cost of the flight, you can redeem points for a free flight on Southwest with as little as 2,671 points. Below is a points redemption view on Southwest Airlines for a flight from Dallas, Texas to Chicago, Illinois.

Sun	Mon	Tue	Wed	Thu	Fri	Sat
				1 3,341	2 4,680	3 2,671
4 4,647	5 3,341	6 2,671	7 2,671	8 3,341	9 6,690	10 2,671
11 4,647	12 3,341	13 2,671	14 4,077	15 4,680	16 8,699	17 4,647
18 4,647	19 3,341	20 4,647	21 4,647	22 4,647	23 8,699	24 4,647
25 4,647	26 4,680	27 8,699	28 4,647	29 4,647	30 6,690	31 8,699

One thing to keep in mind is you can earn points towards redemption on many of the airlines without even flying !! Some of the airlines have partner programs in which the consumer earns points based on registration with a partner. For example; if you change electricity providers, you may be eligible for up to 25,000 points on Southwest Airlines as well as American Airlines. Shopping can also earn you points towards your travel, purchasing from a partner retailer with select airlines can earn you points as well; ordering flowers or e-gift cards are just a few other ways to earn points.

Below is an example taken from American Airlines website.

The AAdvantage Dining Program

Earn up to 5 miles for every $1 you spend

Register up to 6 credit cards to the AAdvantage Dining Program and earn bonus miles each time you pay a bill. New members that sign up and dine will receive a new member bonus. Here's how:

* Register your credit card and dine = 1 mile per $1

* Register your credit card and subscribe to emails = 3 miles per $1

* Dine 12 or more times and become a VIP member = 5 miles per $1

Ballin' On A Budget Question

How many times have you traveled in the past year? Think about how much you could have saved by being a part of a rewards program. Compile a list of the Brands you have traveled with (Airlines, Rental Cars, Hotels.. etc.)

_____

_____

_____

_____

_____

_____

_____

_____

_____

_____

_____

_____

_____

_____

_____

_____

Chapter 3 Tasks

- Review your list of past travel purchases

- Sign up with each Company's rewards program

- Contact Customer Service to see if you can possibly obtain credit for your flight, hotel stay, etc.

Chapter 4

RESTAURANT DISCOUNTS

Dining out can add up to a huge expense you never expected. Who doesn't like to grab a bite to eat, it's quick and there is no hassle of going to the grocery store or cooking. We have to realize even the occasional trips to fast food restaurant such as McDonalds/Burger King..etc. will add up. Five dollars here, four dollars there, by the end of the month, we've spent hundreds of dollars eating out, which of course is not in your budget. So what do you do?.. It's virtually impossible to tell yourself you will never dine out, but there are ways to be smart about it. How many times are we meeting our friends or coworkers for dinner ? Think before you say yes.. ask yourself "Can I Afford this?"

There are ways to be smart when dining out, let's say you want to set aside $100 a month to hang out with friends for an occasional bite to eat. Suggest Happy hour instead of dinner, one thing you will find is many restaurants have 'happy hour' specials.

Sometimes you can order a dinner menu item for the happy hour price. This is one way you can still enjoy dining out while, *Ballin' on a Budget.*

Check out a few of my restaurant favs and the comparison to eating at happy hour vs. dinner.

- Ruth Chris
- Del Frisco's
- Kona Grill
- Pf Changs
- TGI Fridays

- The Cheesecake Factory
- Grand Lux
- Chili's

Let's take for example the menu at Ruth Chris Steak House, which is not cheap for dinner. Ruth Chris offers an $8 happy hour in which some of the items are full dinner menu items. If you opt for a later reservation/dinner you could end up paying double for the same exact item/proportion. Anytime you are spending money, you have to be smart and ask yourself 'is there a way to save' !!

Ruth Chris: *Seared Ahi Tuna*

Happy Hour	Dinner
$8	$17

Eating just an hour or so earlier saves you $9, nearly half the price.

Let's view another example from **Kona Grill**;

Flatbread Pizza

Happy Hour	Dinner
$6.75	$13

Taco Trio

$6.75	$12.25

Chicken & Shrimp Lettuce Wraps

$6.75	$12

Ballin' On A Budget Question

What restaurants do you frequent? Do they offer happy hour? Compile a list of the restaurants you eat at & do your research, see how much you can save by dining on the happy hour menu.

_____

_____

_____

_____

_____

_____

_____

_____

_____

_____

_____

_____

_____

_____

Chapter 5

DIY PAMPERING OR WITH A DISCOUNT

Personal care often falls in the top 3 expenses of the Wants category. Keeping your appearance up often comes with a hefty price tag. There are many ways to save when it comes to your personal care, one way is DIY- Do It Yourself!!

If you have ever been in a financial bind or trying to meet a savings goal, there are things you will have to sacrifice. frequent visits to the hair salon or nail shop may be one of them.

For those who prefer the bi-weekly manicure, which typically cost $30, turning into a DIY-er can save you up to $60 a month !! Now if you are including the pedicure on a bi weekly basis as well, that may run you another $30 every two weeks. Keeping up your own manicure and pedicure can be a savings advantage in the long run. Let's say you spend $120 a month on a bi-weekly manicure & pedicure, when we look at financial perspectives, this is a nice chunk of what can boost your savings.

$120 per month x 12 Months = $1,440

Hair care is the next expense under personal care, how much are you spending per month for your haircut/style. Women often bite the bill in this category with a hair appointment costing upwards of $50-100 per visit compared to the gentlemen's $20 haircut.

Now we all aren't as talented to cut our own hair, but if you are, consider this DIY option to save you money.

If you missed the talent train on hairstyling, you still have an opportunity to save in this area. Discount days are a major way to save when having to shop, no matter if it's for your personal care or grocery shopping. When it comes to personal care & grooming, coupons and discounts rarely come to mind. Personal care is still a service in exchange for money, so don't walk around with the misconception that discounts are not available.

Personal care is considered; Manicure, Pedicure, Haircut, Facial, etc

Check with your provider to see if there are discounts you may take advantage of, especially if you are a regular customer. If there are discounts available, try to schedule around the 'discount days' to maximize your savings.

For example, ladies who enjoy a manicure/pedicure, try to schedule your appointment on the discount days where your provider offers maybe 20-30% off, I've seen discounts as much as 50% off for booking on a particular day of the week.

 These savings add up and will allow you to contribute more to your personal savings account and spend less in the wants category.

Ballin' On A Budget Question

How much are you spending per month on personal care? Are you willing to sacrifice some of your personal care to meet your savings goal? Does your provider offer coupons or discount days?

_____

_____

_____

_____

_____

_____

_____

_____

_____

_____

_____

_____

_____

_____

Chapter 6

DOLLAR STORE ADVANTAGE

When money is tight or you are trying to reach a savings goal, you may start looking for ways to penny pinch. Dollar Stores are a great way to not only save money but still obtain some of the same brands as you would in a major retailer store such as Walmart or Target.

If you have never visited a dollar store, you are truly missing out. There are stores such as Dollar Tree, the 99 cent store and more, where EVERYTHING in the store is only $1 !! Items seen in the dollar store have been; name brand dish soap, personal products, cleaning décor & more. Take a trip to your local dollar store and see how much you will save when comparing your shopping list to major retailers.

Here is a listing of true dollar stores (where items are $1)

- Dollar Tree

- 99 Cent Only Store

Below are discount dollar stores (Items are cheaper than major retailer but may be higher than $1)

- Family Dollar

- Dollar General

See Below for the Dollar Store treasure hunt comparison

Suppose this was your shopping list for one store visit

Item	Dollar Tree	Walmart	Target
Reynolds Wrap Alum. Foil	$1.00	$2.49	$2.98
Lysol Multi Surface Cleaner	$1.00	$2.97	$3.14
Colgate Toothpaste	$1.00	$2.47	2.97
Palmolive Dish Soap	$1.00	$2.47	$3.79
Glad trash bags 15ct	$1.00	$3.72	$3.77
Total	**$5.00 + tax**	**$14.12 + tax**	**$16.65 + tax**

**Dollar Tree total is only 1/3 of the other totals **

If you are shopping for household items on a regular basis, these 5 items alone would save you at least $10. You may think $10 is not a big savings but let's use this average savings of 2/3 from the above chart.

If your bill at Walmart or Target is costing you $50 per month for household items, you may be able to reduce your expense by 2/3 of the total, Using the sample comparison, the $50 bill would average out to $16 by purchasing items at the dollar store.

Price comparison based on local prices and inventory

Ballin' On A Budget Question

What items are you purchasing are available at the 'Dollar Store'? Take inventory of your monthly household, cleaning, grooming items, and see how much your monthly savings adds up.

_____

_____

_____

_____

_____

_____

_____

_____

_____

_____

_____

_____

_____

_____

_____

Chapter 7

YOUR OPINION COUNT$ ..... REALLY

Once you've created the budget, and are sticking to it, sometimes we still find ourselves short on cash. You may not have the time to pick up a second job, but you always have time to give your opinion, why not get paid for it. A quick way to generate additional cash is signing up with focus groups , there are tons of brands ready to launch new products/services and they want YOUR opinion. Focus groups/surveys pay anywhere from $50 -$300 for 30 minutes to 90 minutes of your time, talk about return on investment. If you are new to focus groups, no worries, it is a quick and easy process to sign up. Restaurants will even pay you to try new menu items, a double whammy, you get paid to eat a free lunch. If you choose to go this route, be sure to register with more than one company and your chances will increase to being selected for a survey. Once you register, by providing demographic information, (this is how companies choose attendees, depending on their study) age, sex, location, race, income, so many people are selected within each group. Some companies will email you a quick survey to see if you qualify, maybe 5-10 questions, and there are others who may call you based on your registration information, inviting you to a nearby study.

I recommend signing up with the following, although there are many companies, be sure to do your research.. and never provide your information such as your social security # or credit card information, sign up is free.

InspiredOpinions.com

FieldWork.com

FocusFwd.com

FocusGroup.Com

Ballin' On A Budget Question

How much TIME are you wasting each week? Either watching TV or attending happy hour ? Imagine making $200 for 1-2 hours of your time? Compile a list of days/times you would be available to attend focus groups.

_____

_____

_____

_____

_____

_____

_____

_____

_____

_____

_____

_____

_____

_____

Chapter 7 Tasks

- Sign up with at least 2 Survey Companies

- Check Your Junk Mail to be sure you aren't missing out on opportunities

- REPLY to the survey questions, this is how you are found to be qualified.

- GO... don't decline the survey invitation, if you are serious about saving, cancel your plans for the evening and go get this money !!

Chapter 8

AIR B-N-B'N IT

Homeowners, where are you? If you are one of the lucky people who can take advantage of this hack, awesome. If you are still low on cash after the previous savings tips, try renting a room every now and then if you aren't up for the full time roommate situation. AirBNB allows you to list a room for rent or your entire condo//house for a day or multiple days. Let's say there is a special event in your city, of course we all know hotel prices spike up when there is a special event, this is the perfect time to list a room for rent or your entire swelling to make a quick buck. Some are willing to pay hotel prices to have a residence to themselves or even a room that feels like 'home' Try it out but make sure you are insured and have the proper protection for your home and property.   Read up on the terms with the sites allowing you to list your rental and as always be careful, ensure you require deposits, etc. which will cover damages or insurance deductibles.

Check out the options available to you from Air B N B
www.airbnb.com

A few well-known alternatives to Air B N B are;

HomeAway – www.homeaway.com
VRBO – www.vrbo.com

Let's say you were to rent a room 4x a month for $75 per night.
4 Nights x $75 per night = $ 300

If you were more aggressive with renting and choose 10 nights per month.

10 nights x $75 per night = $750

The extra cash can be applied towards your mortgage or added to your savings.

Ballin' On A Budget Question

How many rooms could you potentially rent out? What would you charge per night?

_____

_____

_____

_____

_____

_____

_____

_____

_____

_____

_____

_____

_____

_____

Chapter 8 Tasks

- If you choose to participate through Air B N B (or other forms of rentals) Be sure to read the disclosure on the websites

- Contact your homeowners insurance to see if additional coverage is needed

- Research the laws on obtaining background checks on renters

- Set a deposit amount that will cover your insurance deductible

Chapter 9

CUT THE CABLE BILL....NETFLIX & CHILL

Good old TV, prime time, reality shows, sports, cartoons (Yes, some adults still indulge in cartoons) The things we don't want to give up. Once we are home from a long days work, most of us tend to watch TV. The one hour of downtime to relax from work and rush hour traffic sometimes turns into four hours of your evening, then off to bed. Many consumers are customers of a cable service provider. Your cable bill may be in the top 3 'wants' of your monthly expenses since cable prices continue to rise. The average consumer pays $100+ per month for cable. Think about how much you are spending on your cable bill each month, is it worth it? Actually, paying for Cable TV has become a thing of the past with the abundance of technology we have. If you are trying to cut expenses, the cable bill is a must !!. There are several options aside from paying $100+ a month. Netflix is one of the options out there to watch TV shows and such, although it's not live TV, you can have your TV show fix. Other options are subscribing to the apps via your phone or tablet (HBO , Starz) many of the premium channels offer apps you can download, and you pay a low monthly fee.

Other options would be purchasing usb connection devices such as; Apple TV, Roku or the Amazon Fire TV stick. These three devices have apps built into the systems to allow live TV or recorded TV shows & movies. are other options for TV show viewing ability.

Let's take a look at your possible savings. If you are paying $100 per month for cable, this totals to **$1,200 per year**. Many Americans do not have $1,200 in their savings account. Cutting the cable bill will allow you to have an additional $1,200 set aside for an unexpected expense or emergency.

Ballin' On A Budget Question

How much are you spending on cable? Are you able to live without cable ? How many hours a week are you spending watching TV? Think about the time and money you can save by cutting the cable bill.

_____

_____

_____

_____

_____

_____

_____

_____

_____

_____

_____

_____

_____

_____

Chapter 9 Tasks

- Research cable alternatives

- Are your 'shows' available on Netflix, Hulu, Amazon Fire TV Stick or Roku ?

- Are you willing to give up TV to reach your savings goals?

- Is TV making you money? Unless you answered yes to this question, you'd better have a great reason to keep this bill !!

Chapter 10

I'M A LONG TIME CUSTOMER !

In the previous chapter we discussed 'cutting the cable bill'. Let's say you are one of those people who can absolutely not live without your talk shows, reality TV, etc. There are still ways to be smart about keeping your services. Being smart and budget conscious in regards to your bills stretches further than your cable bill, think about all of your monthly utilities. As a consumer, you may be paying for; cell phone, electricity, gas, cable, internet, etc.

Let's say you've been a long time customer of ABC cell phone company and you are currently paying $120 a month, contact the company to see if you qualify for any type of rate plan change or customer discount. Another option is to threaten to cancel your service, this always works with a few of the cell phone, cable or electric companies. Companies never want to lose a customer to the competition, so sometimes they will budge and either lower your rate plan or give you a credit on your bill.

If you have been a long time customer and your service provider refuses to change your plan or give you a discount, start looking into other options. Sometimes we become complacent as consumers and forget to price match our services, new packages often arise with competitors and it is worth your budget to look into the options.

Remember, every dollar counts when budgeting If your provider is only agreeing to a $20 discount, the $20 adds up!! Imagine if 3 of your service providers gave you a $20 rate plan discount, that is $60 a month in savings.

Ballin' On A Budget Question

How many years have you been with each service provider?
Compile a list of your service providers and how long you've
been with each one.

_____

_____

_____

_____

_____

_____

_____

_____

_____

_____

_____

_____

_____

_____

_____

Chapter 10 Tasks

- Contact each service provider to see if you are eligible for a lower rate

- If you are unable to obtain a lower price, threaten to change providers, ask to speak with a manager

- Research Service Provider Alternatives to save you money !!

Chapter 11

NO SHOPPING !

Are you a shopaholic? Do you run to the mall for the newest pair of shoes or need a new outfit for every event. If you are one of those people who has clothes in your closet with the tags still intact, you can probably give up shopping for a while. How much do you spend purchasing a new shirt or slacks each month? Set a personal goal and tell yourself you will not shop unless there is a special occasion in which you have nothing to wear... NOTHING.   Just because you wore something before does not mean you can't wear it again. Set goal for 6 months, even 1 year where you are not shopping. One year seems like a long time in which you aren't shopping or buying new items but watch your savings grow and your habits change. It doesn't take long to form a new habit, once you curb this one, you will find it less of a need to even step into a shopping center.

Once you have reviewed your spending habits for the past 3 months, how much are you averaging per month shopping for clothing or accessories? Let's say you spend $75 per month, turning the shopping into savings adds an additional $900 per year to your savings *($75 per month x 12 months = $900).* When you are looking for ways to save start looking at what you may see as a minimal expense, a purchase here and there can help out when you are in need.

There are several options available to rent clothing for special occasions, this comes in handy for the person who doesn't want to spend $400 on a dress to a wedding or special event. Research your options to rent vs. buy and see how much you can keep in your pocket.

Check out the following sites for special event clothing rentals.

www.renttherunway.com   www.menswarehouse.com

Ballin' On A Budget Question

How much do you average per month shopping for clothing ?
Do you have clothing in the closet that you've never worn? If
so, what are you waiting for to wear the clothing. Are you
willing to sacrifice the newest trends to be financially
healthy?

_____

_____

_____

_____

_____

_____

_____

_____

_____

_____

_____

_____

_____

Chapter 11 Tasks

- Review the last 12 months of bank & credit card statements, How much did you spend shopping?

- Could any of the last 12 months of shopping be avoided?

- Think about special events, how much could you have saved to rent a dress/suit or outfit instead of purchasing?

Chapter 12

TAKE A RIDE WITH ME

Are your vehicle expenses keeping you from saving? How much are you spending on gas each month? What about car repairs?

Think about carpooling to work or using the rideshare such as Uber or Lyft. These are great ways to not only save on gas but reduce the beating on your vehicle, which will save you money in the long run. If you are using the rideshare apps there will occasionally be coupons available for free rides, who doesn't love free stuff? Why not take advantage? Think about it, a $20 credit may get you to and from an event without you having to worry about gas, the drive and charges for parking. Download Uber & Lyft today and just for you depending on your city, take advantage of up to $50 Lyft credit by using the code **MSUITE (Credit Amount depends on city)**

If Uber is your choice, here is a free ride on me, use the code **pm9x5ue (limitations apply)**

If the vehicle expenses aren't the issue for you, and you are seeking a way to earn additional cash sign up to become a drive for Uber or Lyft. A quick way to earn additional income and you set your own hours. If you want to drive 4 hours a week or 30, it's up to you. The good thing about becoming a rideshare driver, some of the mileage & expenses you incur for your vehicle become a tax write off, eventually helping out your bank account.

Ballin' On A Budget Question

What are your top expenses when it comes to your vehicle? How much are you spending on gas each month? Would public transportation save you money?

_____

_____

_____

_____

_____

_____

_____

_____

_____

_____

_____

_____

_____

Chapter 12 Tasks

- Review your monthly vehicle expenses, compare to the cost for commuting via public transportation or carpool.

- Are you willing to sacrifice the convenience of your car of a few months to reach your savings goal?

Chapter 13

COUPONS

How many times have we received coupons in the mail and never put them to use? Coupons add up !! No matter how small there are, if you are constantly taking trips to the grocery store, etc. and remember you have a coupon at home, wait to purchase, be sure you use the coupon. Now don't get confused, just because a retailer sends you a coupon, this doesn't mean you need to purchase the item. But if you are planning to purchase the item then be sure to use the discounts available. Another option to paper coupons are store apps, many grocery stores are starting to use electronic coupons within their app. Kroger, Tom Thumb, Albertsons & Whole Foods are just a few of the grocery stores who have converted to electronic coupons via an app. Ask your local grocery if there is an app available.

Check out the coupon sites and apps suggested and start a new savings trend for your financial goal.

www.Coupons.com

www.Groupon.com

www.LivingSocial.com

www.RetailMeNot.com

Ballin' On A Budget Question

Review your grocery receipts, was there a coupon available to use? Search the coupon directory and compare to your latest shopping receipt, how much would you have saved?

_____

_____

_____

_____

_____

_____

_____

_____

_____

_____

_____

_____

_____

Chapter 13 Tasks

- Sign up for your grocery store app if available

- Sign up on couponing sites

- Review the weekly grocery store advertisement before heading to the store. Plan your shopping list around discounts and what is needed.

Chapter 14

BARTER LIKE YOUR LIFE DEPENDS ON IT !!

Have you ever needed a service but you can't afford to pay? Have you ever thought about paying for a service with a service? This is called *bartering*. Let's say for example you need your lawn mowed or your car to be repaired and you are short on cash. What could you offer the person in return instead of cash? Do you have a specialty? (Cutting hair, consulting, etc.) Bartering is a major benefit if you are a small business owner, there are many people willing to exchange goods or services without you having to deplete your bank account.

If you are unsure of where to find others willing to barter, try posting online ads. Social media such as Twitter & Facebook have been known to draw a response to service advertisements, there are even groups on Facebook for such exchanges. You may also try posting within your local newspaper or online via s source such as craigslist. On the Craigslist website there is a category specifically for exchanging goods & services.

One thing to keep in mind when bartering, you still want to do your research on the person/business providing services. For instance, if someone is willing to barter with you to fix your car you want to be sure they are skilled in that particular area with reviews which would be acceptable if you were paying them cash.

The following are 'barter friendly' sites to review:

www.craigslist.com

www.u-exchange.com

If you decide to search or post online, remember protect your credentials and use common sense and safety first.

Ballin' On A Budget Question

Do you have a skill or items you can use for bartering? List below what you could offer in exchange for good or services and the dollar value of each.

_____

_____

_____

_____

_____

_____

_____

_____

_____

_____

_____

_____

_____

<u>Chapter 14 Tasks</u>

- Try bartering with someone you know to see how well it works.

- The second go round maybe try bartering by referral, it may be easier to work with someone who knows you before venturing off to exchange with someone you don't know.

- Post an ad to your social media to see what types of responses you receive

Chapter 15

SIDE HUSTLE & BUSTLE

Sometimes throughout life we may find ourselves with few dollar left over to spend or save once our bills are paid. Until we are able to reach the next level in Corporate America or obtain the next big client as an entrepreneur, one way to increase your income is to take on a second job or a 'side hustle'.

Now, what is a side hustle per se – a side hustle is a part time job or gig which sometimes varies from what we do for our main revenue stream.

Example; You may have a corporate job as an Accountant but on the side you are a graphic designer, or you style hair, etc.

The side hustles we take on come in many forms and fashions, we must remember to use our talents wisely. If you are struggling to make ends meet, think of your skillset and how you can put it to use to create a side hustle. You don't even have to create a position, some choose to work part time at a retail store, sell products such as Mary Kay, etc.

Whatever you choose to do, be sure to incorporate this income into your budget. Some people will call the money brought in from a side hustle, their *play money,* this is also income !! No matter where the money is coming from, it should be a part of your budget and split into one of the 3 budget categories.

Ballin' On A Budget Question

What other skills do you possess in which you can turn into a side hustle? Are you willing or able to take on a part time position? Even if only for 3-6 months, are you willing to sacrifice to reach your savings goal?

_____

_____

_____

_____

_____

_____

_____

_____

_____

_____

_____

_____

<u>Chapter 15 Tasks</u>

- Identify at least 3 skills you have that can make you additional money

- Identify 3 part time positions you can possibly in take on to make additional money

- Identify your availability for a side hustle (days, hours, etc.)

- Plan and put in work.. money doesn't make itself !!

Chapter 16

DARE & COMPARE

How many times have you been shopping then only a few days later you see the same item at a substantially lower price? As a consumer, this has had to have happened at least once or twice in your shopping lifetime.

One thing we forget to do as a consumer is compare and price match our purchases. Many times we are in a hurry or we would rather not take the time to research. 30 minutes of research on an item could save you hundreds of dollars, especially if you are purchasing a 'big ticket' item.

Never purchase an item, especially big ticket without comparing at least 2 other prices. Sometimes we as consumers are so caught up on the new purchase, we forget to compare. Even if you want to purchase from your favorite retailer, ask if they can price match the cheaper price, there are many retailers who will price match to keep you as the customer.

Think about any upcoming holidays, can you wait until the holiday sale? We all know retailers have sales every holiday weekend, maybe shop around the holiday ads if you can hold off on the purchase, your pockets will benefit big time !!

Ballin' On A Budget Question

Do you plan on purchasing any 'big ticket' items in the near future? Can you wait for a holiday sale? List out the items you plan on purchasing in the next 12 months, create a timeline of the holidays to check sales.

_____

_____

_____

_____

_____

_____

_____

_____

_____

_____

_____

_____

_____

Chapter 16 Tasks

- Review the last big ticket items you purchased in the past 12 months

- Look up what the prices are now, how much could you have saved if you waited to purchase the item?

- Research one item you are wanting to purchase, check the price at 3 different stores. If you are wanting to purchase from a particular retailer call ahead and ask if they price match other stores or online prices.

Chapter 17

SPRING CLEANING.. YEAR ROUND

If you are one of those people who stick with the rule 'spring cleaning' think about how much money you can save if you cleaned your closet more often. Sometimes we are pack rats and forget the items we have purchased, visiting your closet/storage on a regular basis will eliminate duplicate purchased but also allow you to 'sell' items you are no longer in need of. This includes, household items, clothing and more.

How many closets do you have packed to the ceiling in which you never open? Try cleaning out your closet, and see what can go. Post the item for sale on eBay or within your local community and there you go, you just added to your savings.

Once you clean your closets and identity items to get rid of, you have one of two options to help put money back into your pocket. The first option, mentioned above, sell the items. The money profited can be deposited into your savings account. The second option is to donate to items to charity, your donation will count as a tax write off, savings you money when tax time rolls around. If you choose to donate to charity, be sure to obtain a receipt or letter with the value of your donation.

Ballin' On A Budget Question

Do you have a storage or closet that needs cleaning out? Do some 'Spring Cleaning', list the items you can sell or donate.

_____

_____

_____

_____

_____

_____

_____

_____

_____

_____

_____

_____

Chapter 17 Tasks

- Research the current value of the items you have to sell or donate

- Research websites you can sell your items on & applicable fees

- Research charitable organizations you can donate to (be sure they are non-profit)

Chapter 18

YOU'RE GOING TO NEED A BIG TRUNK !

Sam's Club, Costco, etc. Many believe these stores are only for families and shopping for major events. Buying in bulk actually saves you money in the end, although the upfront bill may seem costly. When you think 'buy in bulk', this is not limited to food, there are only so many food items you can buy in bulk without having the risk of the food going bad. Think about how many things you can buy for your household in bulk to save money;

- Toilet paper
- Toothpaste
- Paper towels
- Garbage bags
- Facewipes
- Deodorant
- Face moisturizer
- Water
- Vitamins

Imagine a 6 month bulk haul, think about how many of these items we purchase monthly and the associated cost. There are even times where purchasing the regular items cost more than the bulk item. Review the cost comparison below and why you should buy in bulk.

Item	Target	Sam's Club
Glad Force Flex	$16.99 (100ct)	$13.18 (140ct)
Quilted Northern Toilet Paper	$25.99 (12 Double Rolls)	$19.96 (32 Jumbo Rolls)
Bounty Paper Towels	$18.79 (12=18 Rolls)	$19.74 (12=25 Rolls)
Neutrogena Face Wipes	$9.29 (2 Packs, 50ct)	$12.93 (5 Packs, 125ct)

Ballin' On A Budget Question

What items can you buy in bulk?

_____

_____

_____

_____

_____

_____

_____

_____

_____

_____

_____

Chapter 18 tasks

- Obtain a membership at a bulk retailer such as Sam's Club/Costco

- Review what items you are purchasing as well as the cost. Price the item items at a bulk retailer to see how much you would benefit by purchasing in bulk

Chapter 19

DO WHAT YOU WANT, WHEN YOU WANT

Very similar to a side hustle, working as a freelancer allows you to use your skills to generate additional income. Many people choose to 'piggyback' off of their background in corporate America. Let's use the accountant position for example, someone working a corporate position as an accountant may choose to 'freelance' as a part time accountant or prepare taxes during tax season for consumer & business clients. Whatever you choose to do as a freelancer, be sure to compare your options. A few suggested sites for to place ads or look for work as a freelancer:

UpWork –Upwork.com

Freelancer – Freelancer.com

Elance – Elance.com

Guru – Guru.com

Toptal – Toptal.com

99 Designs – 99Designs.com

People Per Hour – PeoplePerHour.com

Craigslist – Craigslist.com

Freelance Writing Gigs – FreelanceWritingGigs.com

Ballin' On A Budget Question

What types of freelance projects can you use your skills to work on? How much time can you dedicate to freelancing?

_____

_____

_____

_____

_____

_____

_____

_____

_____

_____

_____

_____

_____

Chapter 19 tasks

- Research a few freelance websites and rates of pay for your background/experience.

- Create a profile on at least 3 freelance websites

Chapter 20

IS THERE AN OUTLET ?

In chapter 11, we discussed giving up shopping for a while. Of course we can't give up shopping forever but we can be smarter and 'Ball On A Budget' Eventually we are going to need a new pair of shoes or a new top once we've worn down our old ones. Outlet malls are the perfect way to save money if needing to buy new clothes or anything for that matter. There are major retailers for clothing, even appliances with outlet centers. On occasion, you may visit an outlet mall and see the same exact dress at the regular mall location for $70 cheaper !! How can retailers do this? It's called *overstocked* items . Any items out of season or over stocked tend to show up on the outlet locations, making it easier on your pockets if you are smart and patient enough for the deal.

Outlet malls are not only for clothing, many appliances can be found for steep discounts at outlet retailers. Sears is well known for outlets across the U.S. If you are a seeking new appliances (Washer, Dryer Dishwasher Refrigerator, etc.), you may want to visit a Sears outlet near you to do a price comparison.

Listed below are a few major retailers known to have an outlet location:

Nike

Sears

Bath & Body Works

Saks Fifth Avenue

The Children's Place

Ballin' On A Budget Question

Think about your favorite retailers, do they have an outlet ?
Visit an outlet location, compare how much you would spend
on a top, pants and pair of shoes vs. the regular retail
location. For the person obsessed with appliances, compare
the price of a refrigerator , dishwasher, and washer dryer..
how much can you save?

_____

_____

_____

_____

_____

_____

_____

_____

_____

_____

_____

_____

Chapter 20 tasks

- Look up outlet malls local to you

- Visit a nearby outlet to price compare & see how much money you can save.

Appendix

Notes

Budget Overview Q&A

Be realistic when answering these questions

1. Monthly Net Income (Net is AFTER taxes)

2. Monthly Savings Goal:

3. What is your #1 monthly expense for Needs?

4. What is your #1 expense for Wants?

5. What can you remove from your expenses?

6. What can you reduce from your expenses?

7. Are you loaning money you can't afford to loan?

8. Are you borrowing money you can't afford to pay back?

50/30/20 Worksheet

Use this worksheet to help plan your budget into the budget categories of Needs, Wants & Savings

Needs Not to exceed 50%	
Wants Not to exceed 30%	
Savings Save at least 20% in savings	

Budget VS. Actuals

Use This worksheet as a guide to see your budget on paper.
Write down what your budget is for one month, follow up by
filling in the actual amount spent.

Expense	Budget	Actuals
Example: Eating out	**$50** (You budgeted $50 for the month)	**$100** (You Spent $100 for the month, over budget by $50)
Example: Entertainment	**$50**	**$0** (You didn't spend any money in this category, when below budget, place the leftover cash in savings)

52 Week

Week	Deposit Amount	Account Balance
1 (Starting Point)	**$1**	**$1.00**
2	$2	$3.00
3	$3	$6.00
4	$4	$10.00
5	$5	$15.00
6	$6	$21.00
7	$7	$28.00
8	$8	$36.00
9	$9	$45.00
10	$10	$55.00
11	$11	$66.00
12	$12	$78.00
13	$13	$91.00
14	$14	$105.00
15	$15	$120.00
16	$16	$136.00
17	$17	$153.00
18	$18	$171.00
19	$19	$190.00
20	$20	$210.00
21	$21	$231.00
22	$22	$253.00
23	$23	$276.00
24	$24	$300.00
25	$25	$325.00
26	$26	$351.00

Savings Challenge

Week	Deposit Amount	Account Balance
27	$27	$378.00
28	$28	$406.00
29	$29	$435.00
30	$30	$465.00
31	$31	$496.00
32	$32	$528.00
33	$33	$561.00
34	$34	$595.00
35	$35	$630.00
36	$36	$666.00
37	$37	$703.00
38	$38	$741.00
39	$39	$780.00
40	$40	$820.00
41	$41	$861.00
42	$42	$903.00
43	$43	$946.00
44	$44	$990.00
45	$45	$1035.00
46	$46	$1081.00
47	$47	$1128.00
48	$48	$1176.00
49	$49	$1225.00
50	$50	$1275.00
51	$51	$1326.00
52 (End Goal)	**$52**	**$1378.00**

Notes

Notes

_____

_____

_____

_____

_____

_____

_____

_____

_____

_____

_____

_____

_____

_____

_____

_____

Common Budget Questions

Q. How can I save money if I am already living check to check?

A. *Review your expenses to see what you can reduce or remove. You may be spending unnecessary money.*

Q. How do I save & budget with student loans?

A. *Student loans should be a part of your budget. You first want to see if there is any room for payment reduction through your lender, once you have a set payment, be sure to budget this as a NEED. Your wants and savings limits may need to be adjusted.*

Q. How can I prevent distractions from keeping me off budget?

A. *Learn to say no!! You don't have to attend each dinner or social event, simply decline or reply "it's not in my budget". You may also suggest cheaper or options with no expense so you can still enjoy time with your family or friends.*

What Can I Sacrifice ?
Budget Think Pad

_____

_____

_____

_____

_____

_____

_____

_____

_____

_____

_____

_____

_____

_____

_____

_____

_____

_____

What Expenses Can I Reduce?
Budget Think Pad

_____

_____

_____

_____

_____

_____

_____

_____

_____

_____

_____

_____

_____

_____

_____

_____

Ballin' On A Budget
Check Up

Chapter Tasks

Through many of the chapters, there were tasks assigned.
Use this as a guide to completing your chapter task list.

Chapter	Tasks Completion Status
1	
2	
3	
4	
5	
6	
7	
8	
9	
10	
11	
12	
13	
14	
15	
16	
17	
18	
19	
20	

21 Day Budget Challenge

Over the next 21 days record what you gave up each day in your new ways of being budget conscious.
For example, if you typically buy lunch each day and decide to bring your lunch to bring down your expenses, record how much you saved each day.

Day 1	
Day 2	
Day 3	
Day 4	
Day 5	
Day 6	

Day 7	
Day 8	
Day 9	
Day 10	
Day 11	
Day 12	
Day 13	
Day 14	

Day 15	
Day 16	
Day 17	
Day 18	
Day 19	
Day 20	
Day 21	

How much were you able to save in 21 days? What did you give up? Do you feel you can continue to live your life being budget conscious?

Notes

_____

_____

_____

_____

_____

_____

_____

_____

_____

_____

_____

_____

_____

Thank You

I hope this book helped you with your financial goals of saving. I would love to hear about your success using the strategies provided.

Feel free to leave a review of the book via the following channels.

1. Amazon.com/author/missrmba

2. MissRMBA.com

3. Instagram, Facebook, Twitter
(remember to tag @MissRMBA) in the review.

Made in the USA
Columbia, SC
11 April 2018